Other topics covered in this series

Birdwatching
Fishkeeping
Railway Modelling

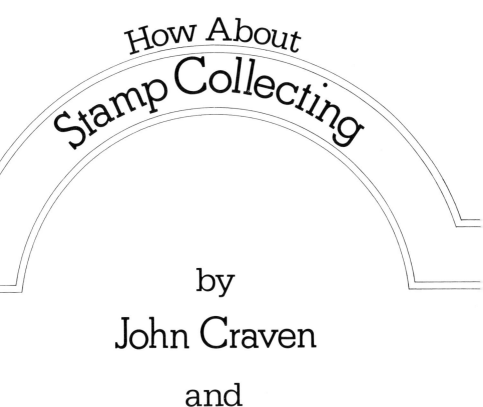

How About Stamp Collecting

by
John Craven
and
Richard West

EP Publishing Limited

Acknowledgements

The publishers and authors wish to thank the National Postal Museum, London, *Stamp Magazine* and Stanley Gibbons Limited for their assistance with this book.
The illustrations were kindly supplied by *Stamp Magazine* and Stanley Gibbons Limited.

ISBN 0 7158 0682 3

Published by EP Publishing Ltd, East Ardsley, Wakefield, England 1979

Contents

Part One by John Craven

The Penny Black 1
What is a Stamp? 4
The Dockwra and the Penny Black 9
Rare Stamps 15
Honouring our Stamps 21
How the Mails get Through 25

Part Two by Richard West

How to Start a Stamp Collection 29
Building up the Collection 34
Developing 39
Stamp Catalogues 41
The Tools of the Trade 45
Presenting your Collection 52
Designing and Printing Stamps 57
Different Types of Stamp 62
Expressions you will Meet 67
Enjoy your Hobby 87
Useful Addresses 88

About the Authors

John Craven trained as a journalist before coming to the public eye with the special news programme for children, 'John Craven's Newsround'. He also appears on the extremely popular children's 'Multi-Coloured Swap Shop'.

Besides being the Editor of *Stamp Magazine*, **Richard West** is a member of the Stamp Collecting Promotion Council and is involved in the organisation of the major British stamp exhibitions. He also serves on the organising committee of the Melville Junior Stamp Competition.

Part One by John Craven
The Penny Black

There, in my hands, was a sheet of paper. At face value, it was worth 240 old pence (£1). But if ever it were offered for sale—which will not happen—this sheet of paper would fetch at least a quarter of a million pounds! For it was filled with proof copies of the world's first—and therefore most famous—adhesive postage stamp, the Penny Black. This whole sheet of them, kept securely behind combination locks in the safe of the National Postal Museum in London, is the only one in existence.

It has been called the Mona Lisa of the stamp world, but I feel it is nothing like as beautiful. I find it a little ugly. There is nothing artistically appealing about the very first stamp. Had I not known the sheet in my hand was so historic, I might have been tempted to pop it into the rubbish bin!

But then, I was a newcomer to the often-surprising business of collecting stamps, and later I was to discover that many of the most valuable items are far from attractive—it is the stories of how and why they were printed that make them so important.

One of my first surprises was to discover that the Penny Black is not, in fact, all that rare. Sixty-five million of them were printed in Britain in

Mr Tony Rigo dé Righi, Curator of the Post Office's National Postal Museum, holding a proof sheet of the world's first adhesive postage stamp, the famous Penny Black

I

1840 and 1841, and any modern collector can enhance his or her album with one for the outlay of a couple of hundred pounds.

The Penny Black earns its place in history because it was *the* prototype for all the billions of stamps that have been issued ever since. To acquire anything approaching a complete sheet of them, you would need to be a

The Penny Black

millionaire or an incredibly wealthy institution. The Postal Museum has the best collection of them for the simple reason that it is part of the Post Office, which issued the Penny Blacks.

But there is always the hope that some ordinary enthusiast might suddenly stumble across a small sheet of them that somehow got lost well over a century ago. That is the kind of dream that philatelists (that is the correct technical term for stamp collectors) thrive on, and such dreams have occasionally come true.

It was with thoughts like that in my mind that I reluctantly handed back this unimpressive, seemingly over-priced sheet of paper back to the man who guards it, Mr Rigo dé Righi, who is Curator of the museum.

Why collect stamps?

As he locked away his most prized possession, I thought I had better get

2

down to earth again, so I asked Mr dé Righi for his views on why people start collecting stamps.

'Stamps are a very easy thing to collect,' he said, 'because they come in everybody's mail. I'm not talking about the kind of stamps we have on display here, though. I mean the ordinary, colourful ones from all over the world that make up the basis of the average collection.

'But keeping an eye on your morning mail for nice stamps doesn't get you very far these days, unless you happen to have a lot of correspondence from abroad.

'So you really need to start acquiring stamps by swapping or buying them, or badgering your friends and relatives to keep them for you. If you know someone whose firm does overseas business, you might persuade them to look out for unusual stamps.'

As you might expect, Mr dé Righi himself has been a keen collector for many years, and he believes that one important reason for people taking up the hobby is that it does not need very much room!

He explained, 'It's not like keeping animals, for instance . . . a collection of snakes, or something like that. Such a hobby needs space, and specialised attention, and sometimes even a licence.

'Stamps can be put away in drawers or cupboards, and other members of the family who don't share the same interest aren't likely to object to them.

'Unless,' he added with a knowing smile, 'you try soaking too many stamps off envelopes in the washbasin, and litter the bathroom with sheets of blotting paper on which you are drying the stamps out. My wife has complained about that before now.'

They do not have that kind of problem, of course, at the National Postal Museum but the compact size of the place—it is part of the Post Office Complex near London's Barbican—proves that you do not need a lot of room, even for a vast collection.

Mr dé Righi is in charge of about two million stamps, from those first Penny Blacks to the very latest issues. Apart from The Queen's collection, probably the finest collection of British stamps in the world, there is nothing to compare with the display at his museum.

We will be hearing more about that collection later in the book, but first, *just what is a stamp?*

What is a Stamp?

The basic purpose of a stamp is to pay the postage on a letter or package, from anywhere to anywhere. Behind that simple statement is a multi-billion pound business that stretches round the world, covering every country, transcending political strife and even, at times, ignoring wars. For many years, there has been a clarion call among human beings that 'The Mails must get through'. But they certainly will not get through, at least not easily, unless they have stamps on.

Stamps are a very convenient way of paying for postage in advance, and those little squares or oblongs or even triangles of sticky paper can take a letter amazing distances by extraordinary means. We all know about the routine means of delivery, like aeroplanes, ships, railway sorting carriages and Post Office vans, but letters can also be delivered by sledge, camel, bicycle, dog-cart, submarine, and even by a runner carrying a letter in a cleft-stick. That last one might sound like something from an old Hollywood movie, but it does still happen.

Before the Penny Black was introduced in 1840, there were no stick-on stamps for paying postage. Anyone who wanted to send a letter in the years before 1840 had it marked either with a handstamp or in the postman's handwriting. Sometimes the cost was paid in advance, on other occasions the *receiver* of the letter was expected to pay.

As postal charges were extremely high in those days, imagine the anger of someone who was sent a letter that he neither wanted nor expected, and was then asked to pay. He would simply refuse to hand over the money. With the 'cash-in-advance' system of the stamp, the Post Office made sure it *was* paid for its troubles.

Stamps in history and geography

As well as being a sensible means of paying for postage, stamps can tell us a great deal about the political and geographical changes in the world during the last 140 years. Also, with the development of clever designs for stamps, they can tell us something about the artistic nature of almost every country. So, as well as being a humble worker, the stamp has also become a kind of social observer.

In almost every rebellion or invasion, just about the first thing the new leaders do after seizing the radio and television stations is to begin printing their own stamps, and in their own currency. This is the ultimate proof to the people of that country, as well as to the rest of the world, that they are in power.

Quite often, the new regime takes over the existing stocks of stamps, and simply prints its own identity on top of the previous design. A recent example of this was when the Kingdom of Libya was taken over by Colonel Gadaffi and his supporters. They overprinted the Royal stamps with their own inscriptions. The same thing happened in Egypt when King Farouk was overthrown.

The rebellion in Biafra was another tragic story which can be told in stamps. Biafra was a region of Nigeria which declared itself independent, and the result was a bitter civil war in which the Biafran forces were eventually defeated. But, for a while, Biafra issued its own stamps, which

Some stamps issued by Biafra during its short life

were used within its self-proclaimed borders as the legitimate stamps of the country. After all, it was a large area and the people living there needed some method of paying postage.

5

Stamps often reflect rival claims to territory, and classic examples of such a state of affairs are the stamps of the Falkland Islands and the Antarctic Territories. Lots of nations claim slices of the Antarctic, and try to prove the claims by issuing stamps. Britain and Argentina both lay claim to the Falklands, and again they prove it with stamps, each showing that the islands are clearly part of their territory!

But despite the things that politicians get up to with their nations' stamps, the postmen seem to carry on regardless. Relations between the Post Offices of the world have been far less affected by wars and other kinds of hostilities that you might expect.

One expert told me, 'We probably kept contact with the German Post Office during the last war. Arrangements were set up for letters to go via neutral places like Lisbon or Switzerland, and obviously this has to be arranged by both the British and German post offices.

'It is possible to have a crisis between two countries, with all diplomatic recognition withdrawn, yet the Post Offices will still be writing to each other. They go on much longer than almost anything else, though often the mails are strictly censored.'

Away from all the political intrigues and international landgrabbings, stamps have also become a thing of beauty. Stamp design is now a minor art-form, and long gone are the days when stamps depicted little more than the Head of State and the value.

Though the very first pictorial stamps were produced in the last century, it is only since the end of the Second World War that the idea of actually making stamps *interesting* has taken off. Almost every country has issued stamps that celebrate this, or commemorate that, and there is hardly a single subject of human interest that has not found its way on to stamps.

Themes in stamp collecting

Many collectors now specialise in what are called thematics—that is, stamps with a common theme. More of that later, but these people certainly have a vast range to choose from—astronomy, banking, ships, motor racing, dogs, space travel, horses . . . you name it, and there is probably a series of stamps to portray it.

Britain started later than most with pictorial stamps, the first being for the Wembley Exhibition of 1924, and the design was one of Landseer's famous lions, at the foot of Nelson's Column in London.

Great Britain's Wembley Exhibition stamps of 1924

Another surprising thing is that Britain is the only country in the world which, as a normal rule, never puts its name on its stamps. Some countries have left their names *off* for special occasions, but Britain has never put its name *on*. This is despite one of the first-ever rulings by the Universal Postal Union, which was set up in the 1870s to provide a common link between the world's Post Offices. The UPU laid down that the name of a country must appear on its stamps.

During my researches I was told, 'All the other countries have turned a blind eye to Britain's attitude. We have always broken the rules because we made the rules in the first place, as we started the whole business of using stamps.

'On the other hand, the UPU *does* oblige us to use the Sovereign's Head, and that is why there is the Queen's profile on every stamp. If we did not use the Head, then we would have to print the name of the country.'

The vast majority of British stamps bear only the Sovereign's Head and the value. They do not even say 'postage' and 'revenue', which earlier stamps certainly did.

The word 'postage' first began to be dropped from commemorative stamps just after the Second World War, because it gave designers rather a lot of problems. It got in the way, and gave stamps a very cluttered

7

appearance. The Inland Revenue was persuaded that the word 'revenue' was not really needed, either, even though stamps are still used to collect certain kinds of taxes.

Every year, the countries of the world issue between five and eight thousand new stamps. Some of them are printed by the million, others in more humble quantities. There is certainly ample material for modern collectors to work on.

The Dockwra and the Penny Black

In the year 1680, a merchant in the City of London by the name of William Dockwra joined up with a number of colleagues to run a rather unusual undertaking. In fact, they were known as Undertakers, but their mission had nothing to do with caring for the dead.

Instead they were in at the birth of a new concept in communications—they set up a private post service. There already was a General Post Office in Britain, run on behalf of the Crown, but it did not do any house deliveries. People had to send their servants (for only the rich could afford the service) to the Post Office to either send or collect their mail.

Mr Dockwra and his friends decided to end that inconvenience, at least within the confines of the City of London, by operating a delivery service. They charged one penny per letter—getting on for one pound by today's standards—and there was a delivery almost every hour. The business prospered, but not for long. The Duke of York, who ran the Post Office, did not take kindly to other people cashing in, and he forced Mr Dockwra to stop his deliveries. To make matters worse, the Duke copied the idea and set up what became known as the Government Dockwra, but eventually the man who thought up the whole thing was paid compensation.

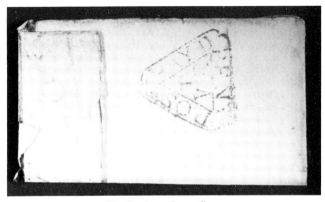

The Dockwra Penny Post

9

Today, there are still just a few of the postal markings used by William Dockwra still in existence. I am told there are probably between twenty and thirty of them, bearing Dockwra's triangular stamp containing the words 'Penny Post Paid'.

Most of these markings are now in archive collections but there are four or five copies in the hands of collectors throughout the world. Anyone who should come across one of them would, quite literally, be able to name his price—should he wish to sell it!

One expert told me, 'The Dockwra Marking is certainly the most desirable hand-stamp there has ever been. His was the first penny post anywhere that still has something surviving to show that it was operational.'

Some years ago, three Dockwras came up for sale. They had been in the private collection of a millionaire who had died. The National Post Museum in London bought the best one for £1,500. The others, not quite as impressive, fetched a little less.

Should they ever come on the market again, the price would be nearer £10,000 each. Dockwras still have a long way to go before they reach the fantastic prices that very rare *stamps* command, but they are beginning to catch up.

Sir Rowland Hill

If William Dockwra and his undertakers were the first people in Britain to realise the sense of a postal delivery service, the man who turned it into a universal means of communications was surely Sir Rowland Hill. He was the man who invented the Penny Black.

Hill was the son of a schoolmaster and he dedicated his life to carrying out various reforms. Among his ideas was a new method of education based on self-discipline, but he will always be remembered for the way he put his brilliant brain to work on the subject of the Post.

The principle of running an efficient postal service was, of course, nothing new. It went back to ancient history for the Egyptians had the first recorded references to a postal system in 2000 BC. One was operating in China a thousand years later, and the Romans with their fine roads and well-organised communications could send messages surprisingly quickly. According to some reports, Roman messengers could travel 170 miles in twenty-four hours—a speed that could not be bettered until the last century.

During the Middle Ages, commerce grew between towns and between nations, and the fact that businessmen needed to correspond efficiently led to the growth of many private postal systems. By the time Rowland Hill was born in 1795 there was a flourishing postal network in Britain, run by the government. As the cities and towns developed, there was an even greater demand for good communications, and that was boosted by the building of much better roads and the arrival of the stagecoach.

Stagecoaches were first used by the Post Office towards the end of the seventeenth century, and when Rowland Hill was studying the workings of the system, it was possible for letters to be delivered to places more than

Sir Rowland Hill

a hundred miles from London the morning after they had been posted. Just about as quick as the Roman messengers!

In 1837, Rowland Hill published his ideas in a work called *Post Office Reform: Its Importance and Practicability*. In it, he put forward the blindingly simple theory that the amount of money that a Government gets from its postal service should increase as the population gets bigger and the country grows richer.

To achieve this, he proposed three things. First the prices paid for postage should *come down*, because high rates meant that only wealthy folk could afford the service. Second, there should be *standard charges*, no matter what distances were involved, because lots of different rates only put up the cost of collecting the money. Third, and perhaps most important of all, he suggested that the mail should be *pre-paid*, and to make that possible he proposed an idea which eventually became the stamp.

At first the bureaucrats predictably kicked up a fuss, but they quickly gave in, and three years after putting his ideas in writing, Rowland Hill saw them come true with the first issue of the Penny Black.

Envelopes—an expensive luxury?

Oddly enough, Rowland Hill believed that the ready-stamped letter sheet would be all the rage, not the stick-on stamp. His reasoning was based on the fact that, until 1840, envelopes had been an expensive luxury. Each sheet had been charged separately by the Post Office, and an envelope had counted as an extra sheet.

So people used a single sheet of letterpaper, which they folded up, and then wrote the address on the outside. But when the Penny Black was born in 1840, the rules were changed, and anything weighing up to half an ounce, no matter how many sheets, cost one penny to post including the envelope.

Because envelopes stopped being a luxury, people used them more, and enjoyed the novelty of sticking on the stamps. The first really practical machine for mass-producing envelopes did not come on to the market, though, until eleven years later. It was put on show at the Great Exhibition of 1851 at the Crystal Palace, and it could make 2,500 envelopes per hour.

In the days of the Penny Black, most of the stamps were stuck on to lettersheets, and many of those letters were kept, not thrown away, by the people who received them. Solicitors, bank managers and businessmen kept them in their filing cabinets. Private individuals kept them for sentimental reasons—maybe they were love letters, or letters from home.

Never before had so many people received so many letters. Sixty-five million Penny Blacks were bought within two years, and most of them were used. So it is hardly surprising that many of those letters still survive today, and 'used' Penny Blacks are quite common.

Conversely, *un*used Penny Blacks are quite rare, and expensive. In 1840, the stamp was purchased to serve a new and exciting purpose, and there was no reason to keep it unused in a purse or wallet.

The Twopenny Blue

Two days after the Penny Black was first sold came its sister stamp, the Twopenny Blue. It was a much prettier stamp, and it is now far rarer, because only six and a half million were produced—one tenth the number of the Penny Black.

Today, Her Majesty the Queen has the finest collection of the Twopenny Blues, whereas the National Stamp Museum claims the best selection of the Penny Blacks, including that Mona Lisa proof sheet of 240 stamps. Altogether the museum has perhaps a couple of thousand proof Penny Blacks.

Proof sheets were the 'test runs' for the new stamp, to check that all was well before they were offered for sale. They had a certificate on the back which said they had been approved for issue. The system is still the same today, and proof stamps are never put to work.

The curator of the National Stamp Museum, Mr dé Righi, told me, 'In the early days, stamps like the Penny Black were not kept by collectors, so the only unused ones that survived were 'part-sheets' of them which got lost—ones that fell down the back of a drawer, or something like that.

'Some years ago, one lucky man opened up an old desk and discovered a part-sheet of Twopenny Blues hidden away. There were about forty of them—it was the second largest multiple ever found and today it would be worth a fortune. Stamps like that are fetching £3,000 a piece as singles.

'Here at the museum we have eleven proof sheets of Penny Blacks with more than 200 stamps on each one. The printers used a total of eleven plates to produce the Penny Blacks, and originally there were proof sheets from every one.

'Unfortunately some of them got lost many years ago, and people kept snipping off odd stamps from the sheets that were left. A hundred years ago, if a younger member of the Royal Family decided to start a stamp collection, the Post Office would present him with a Penny Black. Because the Post Office did not keep used, issued copies of the stamp, the officials would take one from the proof sheets.' Through this and other snippings, the result was that eventually there remained just the one, fully intact proof sheet of the world's first stamp.

And the Postal Museum still had no used copies of the stamp which, when they issued it, revolutionised the way that people keep in touch. Not, that is, until Mr dé Righi went out and bought some.

Rare Stamps

One Cent British Guiana

With billions of postage stamps on the market, it is hardly surprising that the oddities and rarities are the ones that make the headlines. These are the jewels in the very best collections—and the greatest jewel of all is owned by a syndicate of eight investors who jointly own the world's rarest stamp.

They bought it in 1970 for £116,000, and now it is valued at a staggering £350,000. It is the One Cent British Guiana, issued in 1856, and despite its fabulous value today, it started life in a very humble way. In fact, it was not really a *proper* stamp at all.

The world's rarest stamp: the British Guiana 1c black on magenta of 1856

What happened was that, back in the year of 1856, the Postmaster in that remote little outpost of the British Empire on the swampy east coast of South America ran out of stamps. A ship bringing new supplies had failed to arrive, so he had no choice but to have some 'stop gap' stamps printed by the local newspaper, the *Royal Gazette*.

The Postmaster told the printer that he did not want anything special. All that was needed was a simple design, bearing the name of the colony and the cost of the stamp. But the printer decided to add his own touch.

15

Previous stamps for British Guiana had featured the emblem of a ship, and though the printer did not have a copy of that design, he did have a block showing something rather similar. It was of a ship in full sail, and it was used to illustrate one of the regular shipping features in the Gazette.

So, that went on to the stamp as well as the name and the price, and as neither the printer nor his assistants knew anything about stamp design, the finished product was pretty pathetic. The Postmaster must have been horrified as he looked at the One Cent Black, printed on magenta paper. Not only did it look amateurish, but it was very easy to forge. To make sure such things did not happen, he ordered his clerks to initial each stamp before it was sold.

That is how this insignificant bit of paper, roughly printed during an emergency and initialled 'EDW' by some humble clerk, made its way into history.

The newspaper did in fact print two values of stamp—a one cent and a two cent. It is the one cent that is unique, because until now only one copy of it has turned up. It vanished for several years after it was used on a letter and it was discovered by a schoolboy collector named Vaughan in 1873. Later he sold it for six shillings. Now, it is worth more than a third of a million pounds.

That purchase of the One Cent British Guiana is the ultimate in the growing business of buying stamps as an investment. Many purists would argue that such buyers are not genuine collectors at all—they are acquiring stamps for the same reason that others buy famous paintings or Kruger rands . . . purely as a means of protecting their wealth against the perils of inflation.

It certainly seems to be successful. The value of rare stamps has increased enormously in recent years, putting them well beyond all but the richest customers. The stamp dealing firm of Stanley Gibbons produced an 'investment brochure' in 1973, featuring thirteen stamps and including one of the famous 'Post Office' Mauritius 2d blue of 1847 (more about that stamp later on). The whole collection was worth £82,940 in 1973. Five years later, the same collection was worth £268,000!

Of course, no one living in British Guiana in 1856 could have imagined in their wildest dreams what fate was in store for their tatty little one cent stamp. But in our modern world of free enterprise, anything that is rare has a value, the rarer it is the higher the value, and there are few things rarer than that particular stamp. Some collectors may bemoan the commercialism that has taken over the upper realms of stamp collecting, but it is simply a fact of life.

Anyway, there always has been a lucrative trade in the buying and selling of stamps. Even in the early days, there were people who realised that certain stamps could be worth more than their face value.

Stanley Gibbons

Mentioning a moment ago the name of Stanley Gibbons reminds me of the tale of how the famous firm, with its head office in The Strand in London, began—and it illustrates the way in which stamp trading started.

Stanley Gibbons was born in 1840—the same year as the Penny Black—and when he was a young man, he worked as an assistant in his father's chemist shop in Plymouth. As a sideline, he started to buy and sell stamps, and he displayed some of his stamps in a corner of the window.

One day, two sailors walked in and asked him if he bought used stamps. He told them he did, and the men went back to their ship, returning with

Stanley Gibbons

17

a kitbag. When they opened it up, thousands and thousands of stamps spilled on to the table.

They were all triangular stamps from the Cape of Good Hope in South Africa—the world's first triangular stamps. The sailors told Mr Gibbons they had been to a bazaar in Cape Town, and won all the stamps in a raffle.

Cape of Good Hope triangular stamp

The young stamp dealer could not believe his eyes when he saw all these wonderful stamps. He gave the sailors a five pound note for them, and they left highly pleased with the deal. It was an even better deal for Mr Gibbons—he reckoned he made at least £500 from the proceeds of that raffle prize, and the money helped him to move to London and set up his famous firm. To give you some idea of what that hoard would be worth today, a single 1d Cape of Good Hope triangular of 1861 was sold recently for £20,000. Who knows, it might have been in that kitbag!

Post Office Mauritius

For Mr Gibbons, that stroke of luck was the start of one of the greatest success stories in stamp collecting. Even so, I am sure he would have been even more pleased if the sailors had presented him, instead, with a handful of 'Post Office' Mauritius.

These are among the great rarities. Like the British Guianas, they were the stamps of a distant colony, this time an island in the Indian Ocean. They were in fact the island's first stamps, in 1847, and there is a charming story attached to their first day of issue.

The Governor's wife was planning a great social occasion—a fancy dress ball at Government House—and she thought the event would be made extra-special if the envelopes containing the invitations carried the first copies of the island's new stamp.

So that is what happened. The issue was delayed until the day the invitations went out, and even though the ball was a glittering success, it is the envelopes the invitations were in that became a legend. Very few of the orange penny and blue twopence 'Post Office' Mauritius were printed, and they got their name for the simple reason that the words Post Office were printed down the left-hand side. Today, there are only 25 of them known to be in existence. One expert told me, 'The last one sold was not a very good copy, and it fetched £80,000 at auction. At another auction, a penny and a twopenny Mauritius on the same cover (envelope) fetched £150,000.'

Mauritius: first stamps incorrectly inscribed 'Post Office' instead of 'Post Paid'

Canadian Twelve Pence Black

Many of the rarer stamps have intriguing stories to tell, and none more so than the strange tale that befell a Canadian Twelve Pence Black of 1851. It belonged to an old man who lived in a log cabin on the banks of the St. Lawrence River.

One day, he put a rather important legal document into an envelope, stuck on one of the new black stamps, and popped it into his iron strong-box for safekeeping until he could post it.

Suddenly, the door burst open and in came a robber—some reports say it was his nephew, who had fallen on hard times. There was a fierce struggle during which the young man tried to snatch the box.

In the commotion, an oil lamp crashed over, and soon the cabin was in flames. Using all his strength, the old man managed to hurl the box through the window and into the river. The thief made his getaway, leaving the old man for dead. But he crawled out of the flames, and before he died, he told a neighbour what had happened. Later, the thief was caught and punished.

However, the story does not end there. Just over forty years later, the river was being widened where the log cabin had been and during the dredging the strong-box was fished out, still intact. Inside was the 12d black, still in the same mint condition as the day the old man stuck it on the letter. In 1977, a similar stamp was sold for £19,000.

Of course, many rare stamps are made even more valuable because of the romantic stories attached to them. Compare the huge price paid for the One Cent British Guiana with another unique but far less romantic stamp, the Hungarian sideways krajczar of 1868. That is worth only £10,000.

Even so, there are few collectors who can afford even that kind of money to furnish their collection with a jewel. People used to say that philately was a hobby for schoolboys, kings and millionaires alike. When it comes to rare stamps, schoolboys do not stand a chance—and these days, I suppose, neither do many kings! Still, it was a schoolboy who first discovered the world's rarest stamp. There's hope yet!

Honouring our Stamps

Considering that Britain was the first country in the world to issue a sticky stamp to anyone who could afford to buy it, we were remarkably slow at setting up any kind of permanent monument to the postage stamp. Now, at last, we have that in the form of the National Postal Museum in London.

Many other countries were far quicker off the mark—Germany, for instance, established its postal museum in 1872. Britain had to wait almost another hundred years, and then it was mainly due to the enthusiasm of a property millionaire who was also a passionate stamp-collector.

His name was Mr Reginald M. Phillips, and he felt strongly that the nation should have a collection which, in particular, showed the story behind the Penny Black. But for years, the Treasury pooh-poohed the idea. You can almost hear the bureaucrats saying to each other, in the years between the wars, 'Fancy the idea! Spending money on a postal museum—on little bits of paper, on games. Never!'

Anyway, Mr Phillips and his friends persisted, and he made a magnificent gesture. He offered the nation his fabulous collection of British stamps—one of the finest of its kind ever—on condition that the Post Office provided a museum so that the public could see it.

As part of the deal, the Post Office would also use the museum to house its own archives. As they consist mainly of twentieth-century stamps, and Mr Phillips' collection covered the whole of Queen Victoria's reign, the two together made one marvellously complete history of British stamps.

National Postal Museum
The idea was accepted in 1964-5, and the museum opened on a very restricted scale. Then, in 1969, Her Majesty the Queen opened the specially-designed National Postal Museum in King Edward Street, E.C.1, and the public can go there from Monday to Friday.

The curator, Mr Tony Rigo dé Righi, told me, 'We must have getting on for two million stamps, as well as the better part of three thousand original drawings by artists for the design of stamps.

'Some of these are by quite famous people. There's one by Rex Whistler, which is quite valuable as a Whistler if nothing else, but it was a quite unsuitable design for a stamp, and it was never used. Drawing for a stamp is a very specialised art, and he just didn't know what he was doing.

'We also have a drawing by Graham Sutherland, and four designs by John Armstrong which were later included in a retrospective exhibition at the Royal Academy. Designing stamps is an art form in its own right.'

Says the curator 'We have here a vast array of stamps and postal history. The case seems to be that what we haven't got, the Queen has in her private collection. And what the Queen hasn't got, we have! One-off items, or items of which there are only two, seem to be shared between the two collections. If you put them both together, you would have a one hundred per cent history of British stamps.

'The Royal Collection of stamps was really established by King George V. He was *the* collector. He was very knowledgeable by any standards, and I'm told that he used to spend three hours in his "stamp sanctum" every afternoon, and woe betide anyone who interrupted him unless it was an absolute crisis.

'This was his way of relaxing, and he built up a collection which covers the whole British Commonwealth, or Empire as it then was. He spent a lot of money himself buying classic material, and since his day the British and Commonwealth post offices have sent many proofs and drawings to the Royal Collection, which is now in the charge of The Keeper.

'It is, I suspect, the finest private collection in the world.'

If that is so, then the National Postal Museum has one of the finest public collections. The gift from Mr Phillips was valued, at the time, at quarter of a million pounds, and now it must be worth ten times as much. It includes a massive amount of material on the earliest stamps, much of it unique.

The Museum also receives the proof sheets of every stamp issued by the Post Office. They have a certificate on the back saying they have been approved for issue—and while I was in his office, Mr Rigo dé Righi showed me the latest proofs, for a ten and a half pence stamp that had been issued the day before.

As well as the Phillips collection and the Post Office archive material, the museum also houses what is known as the UPU Collection. The UPU is the Universal Postal Union, which was founded under another name in 1874 to supervise the use of stamps around the world. One of the clauses in its convention states that each member country shall send every other member country an example of any new stamps they issue.

That does not apply to changes in watermarks or perforations, but it does to major changes such as design, or colour or value.

The main reason for this is so that countries can recognise each other's stamps, and tell whether or not they are genuine. Britain's share of this UPU exchange is kept by the Museum.

It is reckoned that more than 155,000 different stamps have been issued by the countries of the world in the past century, and that is going up at the rate of about 8,000 a year.

Says Mr Rigo dé Righi, 'The number of new stamps fluctuates every year, and much depends on the Iron Curtain countries which are liable to produce hundreds of different stamps. Britain, on the other had, will normally issue six sets of four stamps as a maximum in a year, apart from any changes in the definitive issue. Generally, it's a total of well under forty new stamps a year.

'Although the Iron Curtain countries issue many more stamps they don't, of course, do it to make extra money. But that is not true of some other countries, especially the smaller ones. It seems the smaller the country, the more stamps they issue, because they make a lot of money by selling them to collectors.

'We acquired our UPU collection in 1965, and we also have a much smaller one compiled before the UPU came into being. It was gathered by the Post Office through the Foreign Office, who sent the British Consuls out to buy them over the counter or wheedle them out of local postal officials.

'In this way, they got hold of some rather super stamps, such as the first issue of the Kingdom of the Two Sicilies in mint condition. They were acquired somewhere round 1858 and put straight into an album where they have been ever since, so they haven't had the light on them.

'We also have one of the finest examples of one of the classic Canadian stamps, and it looks as though it has just been bought over the counter. The colours are superb, yet it dates back to the mid-1850s.

23

'What we are missing, though', he added with a tinge of regret, 'are the stamps before that.'

But any regrets he has can be more than compensated by the 'Mona Lisa' sheet of Penny Blacks and the two million other stamps in the cherished care of the National Postal Museum.

How the Mails get Through

The Merchant of Venice has gone down in history, thanks to William Shakespeare, as the man who demanded his pound of flesh. But in *postal* history, the merchant and his colleagues in Venice are remembered as the first people in the world to run an efficient commercial mail service.

Towards the end of the Middle Ages, the city of Venice was a glittering place. It was the centre of the known world's trade and commerce, with its ships ruling the commercial waves, and its merchants operating a vast network of business enterprises.

Naturally, such an empire needed good postal links, because there were lots of important orders, letters and instructions between customers and merchants. So the Venetians set up their own postal service, and it was so successful that it was later copied by merchants in other cities throughout Europe.

An interesting example of the mail system in those days was the link between some of the great Italian trading centres such as Florence and Genoa with the Champagne area in northern France, where six fairs were held every year. Traders from all over Europe went to these fairs, and a great deal of business was transacted.

So the Italian merchants organised a special mail service from their cities to each of the fairs. The route was carefully worked out, with stopping-places along the way, and the service carried orders, commissions and details of payment. It was an international postal system, but of course it was strictly for business—ordinary people could not use it for sending personal letters.

That had been the case with the posts throughout history. In the early days the Egyptians, the Chinese and the Persians all had systems of getting the orders of the rulers through to their servants in distant parts. They had mounted messengers and posthouses, and the Romans with their great empire organised the service to such a perfection that it was not bettered for 1800 years.

Even the ancient Incas of South America had a mail service, using messengers on foot. But it was not until Europe bloomed after the Dark

Ages, and the demands of commerce took over, that the posts really took off.

When the printing press arrived in the middle of the fifteenth century, the amount of correspondence grew enormously, and in many countries, small private delivery services sprung up to handle the upsurge of mail. One of the most successful services was run by a family called the Taxis, who operated a service throughout Europe in the sixteenth century, using thousands of couriers.

Slowly, these private ventures were taken over by the state. France set up a Royal Postal Service in 1477, and in England, a 'Master of the Posts' was appointed by King Henry VIII to run a mail service along the main roads leading out of London.

The Royal Mail had two ways of delivering letters—by postboys and by King's Messengers. The postboys operated a kind of relay system—one would carry the mails for between ten and twenty miles, then hand them over to another, who would cover the next stage of the route. The Messengers went round the country at much higher speed, with letters from the court or the Monarch. Sometimes they got a special fee for delivering just one letter as quickly as possible—the first 'express delivery'.

When King Charles I came to the Throne, he realised that the Royal Mail was losing a lot of money because he had to pay all the bills! So, he opened up the system to people who could afford the charges—and for the first time, it became a public service.

Later, King Charles II appointed Colonel Henry Bishop as Postmaster-General, and it was he who introduced the first 'stamp'. It was called the Bishop's Mark, and it had the month of the year in the top half, and the date in the bottom, and it was stamped on to the letter, not stuck on. The sticky stamp had to wait until the Penny Black.

At that time, London was becoming the commercial centre of the world, and all the nation's mail was routed through the capital city. Postage rates were charged by the mile, and from London there were six main post roads—to Plymouth, Bristol, Dover, Yarmouth, Chester and Edinburgh. But because London was the chief sorting office, letters often went a roundabout route. A letter from Edinburgh to Chester, say, would have to go all the way to London, adding hundreds of miles to its journey.

But, a few years later, a new system was devised by one of the Post Office's own employees, Ralph Allen, the Postmaster at Bath. He planned a system of 'cross-posts' linking all the main post roads and so connecting most of the towns of Britain without first going through London. It was a reasonably simple, very brilliant idea—and it earned him a fortune.

Later, in 1784, someone else who lived in Bath also had a brainwave that revolutionised the post. His name was John Palmer, he was manager of the Theatre Royal, and he invented the mail-coach. He realised that the best and quickest way of delivering mail along this new network of roads was by fast, well organised coaches which did not carry many passengers but which had plenty of room for the letters.

His first mail-coach left Bath at 5.20 a.m. on the morning of 2 August 1784 and arrived at the Post Office in Lombard Street, London—about a hundred miles away—at 8 a.m. the following morning. These days, that journey takes less than two hours, but then twenty-two hours must have seemed a miracle, and the great days of the mail-coach had begun.

During the next fifty years, the mail-coach service was the pride of Britain. Every night, twenty-eight mail-coaches left London for all parts of the country. Not more than five minutes was allowed for changing horses, and the coaches travelled at an average of ten miles an hour! When a coach was half a mile from a village, the guard began blowing his horn as a warning.

Then, as the coach raced through the village, the guard threw down a pouch containing all the letters for the area. At the same time, the local postman held up another pouch filled with letters to be collected on the end of a long stick, and the guard scooped it up. All this without the coachman having to slow down the horses.

By the standards of the day, the speed was truly amazing—a letter could go from London to Edinburgh—that is 400 miles—in less than sixty hours for a cost of less than a shilling. That famous posthorn blown by the guard had other purposes as well—it warned the keepers of tollgates to open up, because the Royal Mail did not pay tolls, and it also warned everyone else using the road to get out of the way for nothing was allowed to delay the mail-coaches.

Some people did try to stop them, of course. This was the era of the highwayman. The guard was armed, often with a flintlock blunderbuss, to scare off the likes of Dick Turpin—and he also carried a cutlass and a pair of pistols for good measure.

The golden days of the mail-coach lasted almost until the arrival of the

Penny Black in 1840, and the last of the famous London mail-coaches ran in 1846. What put an end to them was the dawn of the age of steam. Trains took over the job of delivering the mails. Not only were they much quicker, but over long distances there was the extra advantage that letters could be sorted during the journey.

It was much the same story with the sea-mails. In the early days, letters were carried by sailing ship and often they took months to arrive, if at all. The first steam-ship to carry mail was the *Sirius* in 1838, just a few years after the first steam *train* took over from the mail-coach.

Other changes came as well. In 1855, the first pillar-boxes were seen on the streets of Britain. Before that people had to take their letters to the post office, or if they lived in London, wait until a collector came round the street, ringing his bell.

Then, in the year 1911, came the greatest ever breakthrough in getting the mail through quickly. A young pilot by the name of Hamel flew his aeroplane from Hendon to Windsor in thirteen minutes, carrying ten thousand letters and postcards. It was something of a stunt to mark the Coronation of King George V, who was himself a great stamp collector. It was also the first airmail delivery.

Now, of course, jet airliners carry mail across the world in just a few days, and letters have even been taken to the moon by American astronauts. Quite a tribute to those merchants of Venice, who first blazed the trail!

Part Two by Richard West

How to Start a Stamp Collection

It is very, very easy to start a stamp collection. Everyone has a few stamps at home, even if they are only the more usual ones which are to be found on everyday letters. A little time and patience spent in careful searching will soon reveal many more stamps. Commemorative stamps from Great Britain on envelopes which fortunately have not been discarded; foreign stamps on letters from friends or relatives overseas, or on postcards sent by those on holiday. Before long quite a variety of stamps will have been obtained.

It is a good idea to quickly tell others that you are interested in stamp collecting. Friends of your parents may find additional stamps for you both at home and at their places of business. Your own friends and relatives will also be pleased to help.

Remember that if your friends know you are collecting stamps, and they are also collectors, they will soon be keen to swap their spare stamps for any of which you have more than one.

Albums

Soon you will feel the need to start looking after your stamps properly: to house them safely. It is sensible to keep your stamps in a proper stamp album. Many beginners make do with any suitable book containing blank pages (such as an exercise book), but these are not ideal for the purpose.

Stamp albums come in a variety of styles, but the more inexpensive ones, most suited to beginners, are fast bound (that is, you cannot remove the pages as you can with a loose-leaf album), and have spaces for stamps from every country in the world. Each page in the album is designed to help you arrange your stamps neatly: sometimes the page is divided into large squares, the idea being that you place one stamp in each square; others have a pattern of small squares printed on the page. These small squares enable you to position your stamps neatly.

While you will want your first stamp album to last you a reasonable time, there is no need to spend too much money, because as your collection grows you will find yourself wanting a better album.

Careful preparation

Before putting any stamps into your album, remember to prepare your stamps carefully.

In most cases the stamps you obtain will be attached to pieces of the envelope to which the stamp was originally stuck. When removing the stamp from the envelope make sure you cut well clear of the stamp itself.

You will receive many stamps on envelopes—be careful how you remove the stamps and never damage the perforations

It is very important that your stamps should not be damaged. This means that the serrated edge round the stamp (known as the 'perforations') must not be cut in any way.

To remove the stamp from the piece of envelope, never just tear the stamp off. The best method to use is commonly called 'soaking' but a better term to use might be 'floating'. You place the pieces of envelope with the stamps uppermost on the surface of a bowl of water or on a damp cloth. Leave the envelopes on top of the water until such time as the stamp can be slid gently off the envelope.

Never be in too much of a hurry. Never force the stamp off the envelope. If the stamp does not slide off easily, leave it to 'float' on the water for a little longer.

Once you have removed the stamp from the piece of envelope, place it on a sheet of dry, clean blotting paper to dry. Again, patience is essential. You should never hurry when you are handling your stamps. They can so easily be damaged, and your collection will be spoilt.

When your stamp is dry, it should be ready for placing in the stamp album.

Deciding the country of origin

One question you will quickly ask is the name of the country which issued the stamp. As John Craven explained on page 7, because the very first postage stamp in the world was issued in the United Kingdom (the famous Penny Black, the world's first stamp, could officially be used on letters from 6 May 1840) it has always been allowed that her stamps need not include the country's name, as long as the portrait of the reigning monarch is included in the stamp design.

Stamps on which you may not be able to recognise the country of issue. These examples come from Austria, Belgium, Czechoslovakia, Greece, Hungary, Spain, Sweden and Switzerland

Therefore if a stamp has no country's name on it, you can be fairly certain it was issued in Great Britain.

Stamps from other countries normally have their name printed on them (there are one or two exceptions). If you have any difficulty recognising the country which issued the stamp, and your parents cannot help, there is a book available called a *Stamp Finder*,which will help you identify those awkward stamps.

31

Handling stamps

By the way, when you are handling your stamps do bear in mind that you should not use your fingers. However carefully you wash your hands, they are always greasy, and can make dirty marks on your stamps.

There are special stamp tweezers available, and you will soon learn how to handle your stamps using such tweezers.

Stamp tweezers

There is only one way to position your stamps in the album and that is to use proper stamp hinges. These you can buy from most stationers. They consist of small pieces of paper, gummed on one side. Later I will tell you exactly how to put your stamp into the album using such hinges, but remember always to use them. Never put your stamps into your album with glue, Sellotape, the edging paper around sheets of stamps or any other form of gummed paper.

Therefore, having 'floated' your stamps, using your tweezers, divide them into their various issuing countries, and place them on the appropriate pages in your stamp album.

Floating stamps off their envelopes

At first most young stamp collectors simply arrange their stamps in rows on the album page. Later—particularly when you decide the time has come for a more expensive stamp album—you can arrange the stamps on each page in a more artistic manner.

The main point is that you have now started your stamp collection: you have a selection of stamps in your album which you can look at and enjoy.

Do take the trouble to look at your stamps. Do not just be content to see how many different stamps you can acquire. Each stamp design can tell a story if you look at it carefully enough.

By enjoying your stamps, you will be surprised how much you can quickly learn.

Building up the Collection

Having started your stamp collection you are going quickly to find that just relying on friends and relatives to give you their spare stamps, or just to use the method of swapping, is not going to build up your collection as quickly as you would like.

A visit to a stamp dealer might now be a good idea. There is probably a stamp shop in your area: if you cannot find one easily, look in your local telephone directory, which should give you a suitable name and address.

Most stamp dealers are very helpful, and will be only too pleased to encourage a beginner, and offer help and advice. If you visit a stamp shop you will notice for sale packets which contain a large number of stamps at moderate cost. These are excellent for building up your collection.

You need not just confine yourself to packets of stamps from the whole world. If there is any area where your collection is particularly lacking, then you will probably be able to buy packets of stamps from that area alone.

Most dealers have on their counters an 'inexpensive' box which contains stamps priced at just a 1p or 2p each. Once again these help you build up your collection at low cost.

Naturally as your collection of stamps improves you may find yourself wanting specific stamps—rather than any stamp in general to fill a gap—and then that same stamp dealer will again be able to help you.

However, before worrying too much how the more experienced collector develops his collection, there is nothing better than forming a general collection of stamps, trying to obtain as many stamps as possible. In this way you will be able to see which stamps you find most attractive and which stamps you find it easiest to obtain.

You may find that, as you progress, it becomes more and more difficult to build up a collection of stamps from throughout the world, and that the stamps from certain countries appeal to you less than others. It may be, for example, that by having a pen friend somewhere overseas, the stamps of a particular country come to you much easier than others.

The idea of specialising

You may now decide to start specialising. In other words, you will want to concentrate on the stamps of a particular group of countries, rather than of the whole world.

There is no need to specialise only in certain countries however. You can choose stamps issued during a certain period of time. Let us say for example that you were born in 1965. Then you may decide to concentrate only on those stamps which have been issued since 1965.

You may find that certain stamp designs appeal to you more than others. You may be a sporting enthusiast, and therefore decide to collect stamps showing sporting scenes. Stamps come in such a wide range of designs that virtually any subject you choose can be represented by stamp designs. Animals, birds, aircraft, flowers, railways, cars, butterflies, famous paintings—these are just a few of the topics which you can find on stamp designs.

You can easily combine another activity with your stamps by collecting those stamps whose designs reflect your other interest.

In recent years there has been a much greater attention focused on collecting stamps by their design rather than just by the country of issue. Such a form of collecting is known as 'thematic', as John Craven explained on page 6.

One point to note is that a missing stamp is not quite so apparent with a thematic collection as with a collection based on the country of issue or the period of issue.

One of the great pleasures of stamp collecting is that it can be varied to suit anyone's individual needs. There are really no 'rights' or 'wrongs' to collecting stamps. You collect what you want in the way that pleases you most. However you can nevertheless gain even more enjoyment by learning from the experiences gained by more advanced collectors.

While it is true that a collection is personal, it is not too long before the urge for completeness which grips all collectors starts to reveal itself.

If you are collecting the stamps of a particular country, there are always a few stamps which seem more difficult to obtain than others. This is when the stamp dealer may need to be approached again. This time you will be wanting a particular stamp from the dealer rather than a packet of many different stamps. If you are fortunate the dealer will be able to

A selection of stamps which show how you can combine your collecting with another interest. Collecting stamps by their design rather than the country of issue is known as 'thematic' collecting. These examples show flowers, butterflies, insects, horses, birds, aircraft, ships, girl guides, tennis—the possibilities are endless

supply the stamp you are seeking.

If you establish a relationship with a local stamp dealer, you will find he will be only too pleased to help you develop your collection, and will not charge you more than absolutely necessary for the stamps with which he supplies you.

Sharing with others

Stamp collecting is a personal hobby. You can collect what you want in the way you want. Equally you can share your hobby with others, or you can choose to collect on your own.

When you are just beginning there is much to be gained by sharing your enthusiasm with others; not only swapping stamps with your own friends, although this does help. Perhaps your school organises its own stamp club. This will bring you into direct contact with those at your school who are also stamp collectors; will give you more people with whom to swap. You will also be able to learn more from those who have been collecting longer than yourself.

Your local stamp dealer will be pleased to give you more help and encouragement, although remember he may sometimes be very busy and not able to spend as much time with you as he would like.

A school stamp club enjoying discussing and looking at each other's stamp collections

37

Mentioning at home that you are collecting stamps may reveal a friend of your parents or a relative who already collects stamps, and who would be pleased to give you as much encouragement as possible.

In your area there may be a stamp club (sometimes called a philatelic society). This is a society of enthusiastic stamp collectors who meet say once or twice a month, not only to share their own experiences, but also to listen to someone speaking about stamps and showing part of their own collection.

Sometimes the collections of older collectors may look a little frightening. You feel you could never reach the same level as these collectors.

Never be put off. Remember they have been collecting far longer than you, and have built up the experience which you too in time will gain. They were once beginners and started their stamp collecting in just the same way as you are now.

You can learn from these older collectors. They will be pleased to share their knowledge with you—and maybe also give you some of their spare stamps to help you on your way.

Many societies operate what is known as an 'exchange packet'. This is a way in which members can sell any surplus stamps they may have, while the other members have the chance to buy these stamps.

You may be able to look through the society's exchange packet, and perhaps be allowed to buy one or two of the stamps which you feel you would like.

You will be able to enjoy your stamp collecting if you learn from others, and share your hobby with others.

Developing

You have started your stamp collection by keeping all the different stamps that come your way, and putting them in a fast bound stamp album.

You have been able to decide which stamps you find most attractive and may therefore have determined to narrow your collecting interests and to start specialising.

If you do want to specialise, there are many different ways in which you can do so. You have already been told about the possibility of thematic collecting, where you will be more concerned with the designs of your stamps than with the countries of issue.

You may want to collect stamps with some political or geographical connection. At one time it was very popular to collect the stamps of the British Commonweath, although today even this would prove to be a mammoth undertaking. Why not confine yourself even more? Collect, for example, the stamps from the islands in the West Indies or those of the Mediterranean islands.

You could just collect the stamps of one country. Even to build a straightforward collection of stamps from certain countries would prove to be quite an exacting task.

Therefore you may further confine yourself to a particular period of time. For example, you could choose to collect the stamps of Australia issued during the reign of King George VI.

Some collectors limit themselves even further, forming a collection around just a few stamps or even one stamp.

Never fall into the trap of believing that because two stamps may look very much alike that they are identical. Changes can occur in design (sometimes very minute changes), to the value, to the shades of colouring, and to other aspects involved with the printing of the stamps.

What will be the cost?

When making up your mind about specialising, you may find it worth-while not just to rely on the fact that certain stamps look more attractive to you. Take a look at the stamp catalogues. These will show you what stamps have been issued by any country. You will then be able to see just how many stamps you might need to obtain if you hope to collect a particular country. More important it will give you some idea as to how much these stamps will cost you.

There is not much point in deciding to collect the stamps of a certain country, based on your liking for a few of the stamps already in your possession, if it is going to be almost impossible to add to your collection because so few stamps have been issued or those available are expensive.

A possible foundation

Many collectors, once they have decided on the area they are going to collect, buy an already established collection of those stamps on which they can build.

Stamp dealers often have old stamp collections for sale—or such collections can be bought through auction. They are frequently very good value for money and provide an excellent foundation on which you can build your collection.

Buying such a ready-formed collection might be beyond your pocket, but maybe it could be a present from your parents at Christmas or for a birthday.

Having decided you wish to specialise, you will find that you are no longer content with a fast-bound stamp album, and simply putting your stamps on each album page in rows.

The time has come to change to a loose-leaf stamp album. Perhaps even one in which all the leaves are blank, except for a fine grid pattern to enable you to arrange your stamps on each page in an attractive pattern.

You will want to present your stamps in a more logical way, to find out more about your stamps. You will find yourself needing more equipment, apart from tweezers and stamp hinges. The next few chapters should help you.

Stamp Catalogues

One of the most essential books for a stamp collector is a stamp catalogue. Catalogues come in many forms, depending on exactly what stamps they list, and vary greatly in price.

The most useful catalogue is without question *Stamps of the World* published by Stanley Gibbons. This catalogue is frequently known as the 'Simplified' because it comprises a simplified listing of every postage stamp issued throughout the world. It does not bother with the more specialised differences between stamps, but each basic postage stamp, whatever the stamp, will be recorded.

Indeed, if you have a stamp and cannot find it listed in the catalogue, it is probably not a 'postage' stamp, that is not a stamp issued by a Post Office to denote the postal charges on a letter or parcel. Stamp-like labels are produced for a number of reasons, some of them even claiming to be postage stamps, but unless they have been genuinely released by a Post Office they will not be listed in the catalogue.

If you are looking for the listing of a particular stamp in the catalogue, first you will need to know the country that issued the stamp. Next you will have to look through the pages devoted to that particular country until you find illustrated a stamp similar to that which you are trying to identify. It is naturally impossible for the catalogue to illustrate every single stamp, but normally one stamp from each set is depicted. You will find it easy to identify any stamp from the basic illustrations given.

When you have located the basic illustration, the catalogue will now give you some extra information.

Most stamps are issued in sets, frequently commemorating some event, illustrating a particular theme, or honouring a famous person. The catalogue will list all the stamps which were issued in the particular set of which you have an example.

It will tell you the reason why the stamps were issued, the year in which they were issued (sometimes even the exact date of issue), the denominations of the stamps in the set, and the colours in which each of the stamps was printed.

182. Conference Emblem.

(Des. Reynolds Stone (emblem, P. Rahikainen).)
1960 (19 SEPT.). *First Anniv. of European Postal and Telecommunications Conference*. *Chalky paper.* W **179**. P 15 × 14.
621 **182** 6d. bronze grn. & purple .. 8 6 .. 8 6
622 ,, 1s. 6d. brown-amb-blue .. 20 0 .. 20 0

183. Thrift Plant.

184. " Growth of Savings ".

185. Thrift Plant.

(Des. P. Gauld (2½d.), M. Goaman (others).)
1961 (28 AUG.). *Centenary of Post Office Savings Bank. Chalky paper.* W **179** (*sideways on 2½d.*). P 14 × 15 (2½d.) or 15 × 14 (others).

I. " TIMSON " Machine.
II. " THRISSELL " Machine.

	I.		II.	
623 **183** 2½d. blk. & red	2 6	2 0	10 0	10 0
624 **184** 3d. orge.-brn. & violet	2 0	1 6	4 0	1 6
a. Oran.-brn. omitd. —			—	—
x. Perf. through side sheet margin .. 70 0				†
xa. Orge.-brn. omitd.—				†
625 **185** 1s. 6d. red & blue .. 17	6	17	6	†

2½d. TIMSON. Cyls. 1E-1F. Deeply shaded portrait (brownish-black).
2½d. THRISSELL. Cyls. 1D-1B or 1D (stop)-1B. Lighter portrait (grey-black).
3d. TIMSON. Cyls. 3D-3E. Clear, well-defined portrait with deep shadows and bright highlights.
3d. THRISSELL. Cyls. 3C-3B or 3C (stop)-3B (stop). Dull portrait, lacking in contrast.

NOTE. Sheet marginal copies *without* single extension perf. hole on the short side of the stamp are always " Timson ", as are those with large punch-hole *not* coincident with printed three-sided box guide mark.
The 3d. " Timson " perforated completely through the right-hand side margin came from a

relatively small part of the printing perforated on a sheet fed machine.
Normally the " Timsons " were perforated in the reel, with three large punch-holes in both long margins and the perforations completely through both short margins. Only one punch-hole coincides with the guide mark.
The ' Thrissells " have one large punch-hole in one long margin, coinciding with guide-mark, and one short margin imperf. (except sometimes for encroachments).
A very small quantity of all values was sold in error at the Chorley, Lancs., P.O. on 21st August, 1961.

186. C.E.P.T. Emblem.

187. Doves and Emblem.

188. Doves and Emblem.

(Des. M. Goaman (doves, T. Kurpershoek).)
1961 (18 SEPT.). *European Postal and Telecommunications (C.E.P.T.) Conference, Torquay. Chalky paper.* W **179**. P 15 × 14.
626 **186** 2d. orge., pink & brown 1 3 .. 1 3
627 **187** 4d. buff, mve. & ultram. 4 0 .. 4 0
628 **188** 10d. turquoise, pale green and Prussian blue .. 7 6 .. 7 6
a. Green omitted ..
b. Turquoise omitted ..

189. Hammer Beam Roof, Westminster Hall.

190. Palace of Westminster.

(Des. Miss F. Jaques.)
1961 (25 SEPT.). *Seventh Commonwealth Parliamentary Conference. Chalky paper.* W **179** (*sideways on 1s. 3d.*). P 15 × 14 (6d.) or 14 × 15 (1s. 3d.).
629 **189** 6d. purple and gold .. 4 0 .. 2 6
630 **190** 1s. 3d. green and blue .. 15 0 .. 15 0

191. " Units of Productivity ".

192. " National Productivity ".

193. " Unified Productivity ".

(Des. D. Gentleman.)
1962 (14 NOV.). *National Productivity Year. Chalky paper.* W **179** (*inverted on 2½d. and 3d.*). P 15 × 14.
631 **191** 2½d. deep green and carmine-red (*shades*) .. 1 9 .. 1 3
p. One phosphor band 3 6 .. 2 0
632 **192** 3d. light blue and violet 3 0 .. 1 6
a. Queen's head omitted .. £300
p. Three phosphor bands .. 4 0 .. 3 6
633 **193** 1s. 3d. carmine, lt. blue and deep green 17 6 17 6
a. Queen's head omitted ..
p. Three phosphor bands .. 30 0 .. 22 6

Small quantities of each value (approx. 60 × 2½d., 350 × 3d. and 20 × 1s. 3d.) were sold in error at a Lewisham, London post office on October 16th and 17th, 1962.

194. Campaign Emblem and Family.

195. Children of Three Races.

A page from a typical 1960s stamp catalogue; the style has remained the same

Some catalogues will give you even more information: the name of the person who designed the stamps; the name of the printer and the process used for printing; and it will tell you about such aspects as watermarks and perforations.

The most important information however tells you how many stamps you need to complete any set, the date of issue, and the reason for issue.

Definitive stamps

If, incidentally, no reason is given for the issue of some stamps, it could be because they are 'definitive' stamps. These are stamps which are on sale for a long period of time, as opposed to 'commemorative' stamps, which are sold for just a limited period. The stamps of Great Britain which feature just the Queen's portrait and denomination are the definitive stamps.

Pricing

There is of course a further piece of information which the catalogue gives—the pricing. After the details of each stamp come two prices. That in the left-hand column is for the stamp in unused condition. An unused stamp is one which is as issued by the Post Office. It has not been on a letter through the post and therefore has not been postmarked.

The right-hand column of prices is for stamps in used condition. That is stamps which have been on mail sent through the post, which have therefore been postmarked.

These two columns of prices are usually those at which the publishers of the catalogue will sell you the stamps. They are used as a basis by dealers in deciding what prices they should charge for stamps.

They are not the prices which you would receive for your stamps if you were to sell them. Always remember that when you sell stamps to a dealer, he has to spend time sorting out the stamps to sell again, and must make a profit in order to maintain his business and to live. For many low-priced stamps, the price stated in the catalogue and the price charged by the dealer is virtually fully accounted for by the costs involved in handling the stamps.

Never reach the conclusion that the prices given in the catalogue tell you the 'value' of your collection. A catalogue is a dealer's price list. Use it for the background information it gives you about your stamps and as an indication of what you might be expected to pay if you were to buy any of the stamps.

Condition

This is a good time to mention the condition of stamps. The stamps for which dealers quote prices, and indeed the stamps they will sell you, will be in good condition. That means the stamps should not be damaged in any way—not torn, or made thin by having a stamp hinge or other piece of paper torn badly from the back of the stamp. Used stamps should have a neat, yet clear, postmark that does not obscure the stamp's design.

Naturally, with more expensive stamps, you may not be able to obtain a stamp in perfect condition straightaway. In such cases you could put a less perfect stamp in your collection until such time as you are able to secure a better example.

Other catalogues

So far mention has only been made of the *Stamps of the World* catalogue, but there are many more available. There are simplified checklists of the stamps of Great Britain, Channel Islands (Guernsey and Jersey) and Isle of Man. Catalogues that cover British Commonwealth (all reigns or just the reign of Queen Elizabeth II), European countries and the rest of the world.

The catalogues vary in the amount of information they give. The absolute specialist in the stamps of Great Britain may well need to consult the *Great Britain Specialised Stamp Catalogue*, which runs into four volumes!

If you look at stamp catalogues offered by booksellers you may be slightly put off by the cost. However, public libraries (or your school library) have copies of catalogues available on loan. You may find it possible to buy an out of date calogue at very low cost. Since most catalogues are published each year, and dealers do not really want to stock an out of date catalogue, it is possible to buy a catalogue, only a year old, at a reasonable price.

Used sensibly, the stamp catalogue is the most essential book a stamp collector can have.

The Tools of the Trade

To enjoy stamp collecting you need more than just stamps. Here are a few of the items you will find useful.

Stamp albums

Stamp albums come in a variety of styles—and prices. For the beginner the ideal album is fast-bound—that is the pages are bound together by

A range of stamp albums

staples or by sewing as in a normal book (like the one you are now reading). Such albums have pages which are headed with the names of the world's countries, and you place each stamp on the appropriate page.

Later you may decide to use a loose-leaf album. This is an album where the pages are kept in a binder in such a way that enables them to be easily removed, or new pages to be easily added.

The leaves are held in the binder in a number of ways. Sometimes the binders have a spring mechanism which grips the pages in place. Others use a peg arrangement, there being holes in the album pages that fit on to pegs in the binder. Some have a system of rings, these rings passing through holes in the album pages.

The ring system has an advantage that it allows your stamp album to lie flat when opened: this is not usually possible with other loose-leaf stamp albums.

It is normal with loose-leaf stamp albums for the stamps to be mounted on one side of each page only.

The pages in a loose-leaf album can still be obtained with various country names printed at the top, as with a fast-bound album.

However, by the time many collectors have moved to loose-leaf albums they have started to specialise, and it is unnecessary to have such headed pages.

Many collectors simply prefer their album pages to be completely blank, except for a finely printed grid system to help them arrange the stamps attractively on the page. The collector can then put whatever title he likes to each album page.

It is possible to buy an album with leaves blank except for a single country name; these are usually only found for the countries more popular with stamp collectors. It is also possible these days to buy blank leaves headed with thematic titles, such as 'Fish' or 'Ships' or 'Space' or whatever.

If you decide to specialise in the stamps of just one country, it may be possible to buy a loose-leaf album (known as a 'One-Country Album') with the pages already printed to accommodate the stamps of that country. These albums have a space for each stamp issued by the country, frequently each different design being illustrated. Background information to the stamps is also printed in such albums, but rest assured, they deal with the stamps of the particular country in a fairly straightforward way. All you have to do is to mount the stamp in its appropriate space. Such albums obviously make collecting much easier.

The one aspect to remember about stamp albums is that there being such a wide range, you can choose whatever suits your needs and pocket.

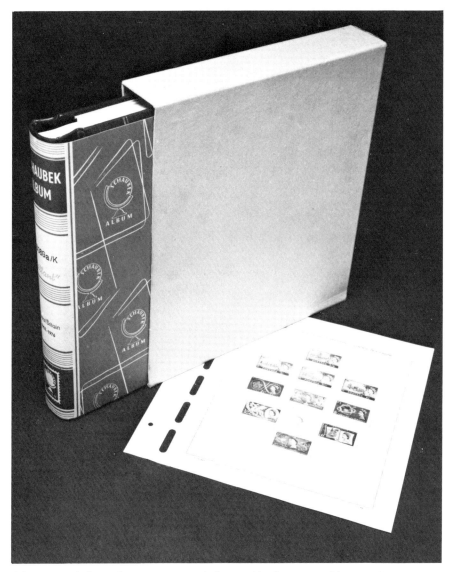

A 'one-country' album where spaces are marked out making it easy to position your stamps

An album designed just to hold first day covers

48

The best idea is to visit your stamp dealer, look through the range of albums available, and buy that which you like most and which seems to suit you best.

Tweezers

Mention has already been made that it is essential that all stamps are only handled with tweezers. It may seem awkward at first, but you will soon become accustomed to them.

Use only proper stamp tweezers—they should have thin ends to enable you to pick up your stamps more easily, but the ends must also be blunt. Sharp edges will quickly damage your stamps.

Stamp hinges

Again use only proper stamp hinges; do not make do with other pieces of paper. The way to put your stamps in the album using hinges is given in the next chapter.

Mention should be made here of a modern idea in stamp collecting of putting stamps into the album using protective mounts which are made of plastic. In general terms, such a mount consists of a plastic pocket in which the stamp is placed. The idea is that nothing is actually stuck to the stamp, as happens with a normal stamp hinge. However, the additional cost of such mounts means they are really only of interest to more advanced stamp collectors.

Magnifying glasses

Magnifying glasses obviously enable you to study your stamps more closely, and to see the fine detail of the stamp design.

There is a wide range of magnifying glasses available, and again it is best to look at the selection available from your stamp dealer, and to select the one that suits you best.

Perforation gauge

The jagged edge to a stamp is called its 'perforations'. The size of the holes can vary, and so collectors want a method of determining the size of the holes on any stamp. A standard form of measurement is based on the number of holes in 2 cm. This means that if along an edge of a stamp there are 14 holes in 2 cm (or equally 14 perforation teeth in 2 cm) then the perforation is said to measure 14.

Because it is obviously not convenient to keep counting the number of holes each time you want to know the perforation of a stamp, special gauges are available which, by matching up the edge of any stamp with the gauge, you can read off the perforation.

The gauge comprises many rows of black dots, each row corresponding to a different perforation measurement, and you place the stamp until the perforations exactly match a row of dots.

Incidentally stamps frequently have a different perforation reading along the top and bottom of the stamp, compared with the reading for the sides of the stamp.

Watermark detector

The design which is frequently seen by looking 'through' a sheet of paper is called a 'watermark'. You can test this by holding a sheet of notepaper up to the light and looking through the paper. A design will usually be seen and this is the watermark.

Stamps often have watermarks. They can sometimes be seen by holding the stamp up to a strong light and looking through the stamp.

However a better method is to place the stamp face down on a black tray and add a drop or two of benzine to the back of the stamp. The benzine will show up the watermark for a short time. Benzine quickly evaporates away.

Special black trays and benzine dropper bottles which release one drop at a time are available from stamp dealers. Incidentally do not use *benzene* by mistake.

There are more expensive methods for detecting watermarks (because some watermarks are very difficult to see, even for collectors with many years' experience) but these are not really of benefit to newcomers to stamp collecting.

Stamp catalogues

Already mentioned, but none the less an essential piece of equipment for any stamp collector.

Colour guide

To help you match up the descriptions given in the stamp catalogue to the colours in which a stamp is printed a 'Colour Guide' is available. Such a guide is particularly important if you find that a particular stamp has been printed in more than one shade of a particular colour. Guides readily available detail either one hundred different colours for general use or two hundred colours for the more specialised collector.

Presenting your Collection

Putting your stamps properly into your stamp album is very important. The term actually used is 'mounting' your stamps. To do this you must use proper stamp hinges, which are tiny pieces of paper gummed on one side only.

Do not make the same mistake as do some stamp collectors in the beginning. If you have an unused stamp with its gum on the back, never simply lick the stamp to stick it to your stamp album page. Also never use any other type of glue to affix the stamp to your page.

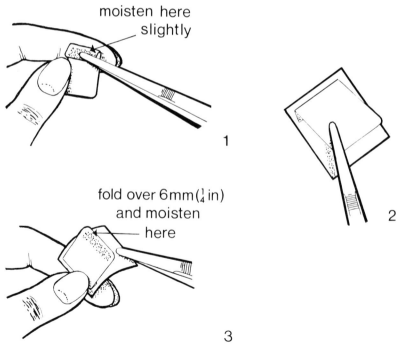

Preparing a stamp for your collection

Only use the proper stamp hinges which are available from most stationers, and of course from stamp shops. Stamp hinges are very easy to use, and you will quickly find it simple to mount your stamps with them.

To mount a stamp you fold the stamp hinge so that you divide it into two parts, roughly in the ratio of one third to two thirds. Gently moisten the smaller part and attach this portion to the back of your stamp. You should place the hinge as close to the centre of the top of the stamp as possible, but making sure you keep the hinge off the stamp's perforations. Incidentally, you should be able to do all these operations using your stamp tweezers.

Holding the remaining portion of the hinge up away from the stamp gently moisten the bottom half of this part of the hinge.

Do remember to hold the hinge away from the stamp and to apply the moisture very gently, otherwise you may find some moisture falls on to the back of the stamp itself. If it is an unused stamp, this will mean the stamp will stick firmly by its own gum on to the album page and when you come to remove it you will damage the stamp.

Having moistened the bottom half of the hinge, use your tweezers to hold both the stamp and the hinge. Carefully position the stamp in its required space on your stamp album page and gently press the stamp in place using a piece of paper (remember you should never touch your stamps with your fingers).

Once you have positioned your stamp you should be able to lift it up using your tweezers to examine the back. If you have placed your hinge just below the perforations there should be no question of damaging the perforations of the stamp when you lift it in this way.

Some stamp collectors these days do not use the type of stamp hinges already described. They use a special type of stamp mount which consists of a plastic pocket into which the stamp is placed. The idea of these so-called protective mounts is that nothing is actually stuck to the back of the stamps. While such hinges may be fine for more experienced collectors, particularly if they have expensive stamps, such mounts are not really suitable for a beginner. They are also much more expensive than the ordinary paper hinges.

The next question to ask yourself is exactly where to position your stamps on the album page. If you are using an album where the names of countries are printed at the top of each page, and there are squares printed on the page itself, then you have little to worry about. You will be quite happy to mount a stamp in each square provided, remembering to check that the country of origin of the stamp you are mounting is in fact the country whose name is printed at the top of your album page.

If you are using one of the 'one country' albums, where all the pages are laid out for you with positions marked as to where each stamp should go, once again you will have no problems. Simply mount the correct stamp in the space provided.

However, you might have progressed to the type of stamp album where each page is completely blank, except for a pattern of tiny squares. Now the arrangement of your stamps on this page is entirely up to you.

You could simply start at the top left-hand corner of your page, and keep mounting your stamps in rows, without any consideration for the size, shape, denomination or date of issue of your stamps.

More experienced collectors prefer to arrange their pages much better than this, so that each looks as attractive as possible.

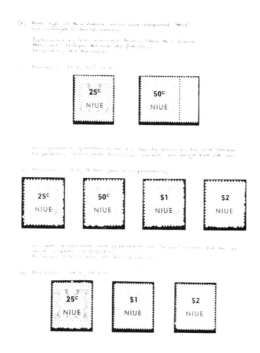

A carefully arranged page of stamps. Note that the page is not overcrowded with stamps and the stamps have been well balanced to produce a pleasing effect

Naturally you will be influenced by the extent to which your collection has grown. If you have decided to specialise then the stamp catalogue will show you how to divide your stamps into sets.

A set is a group of stamps issued by a particular country for one reason, such as to commemorate a certain event: normally all the stamps in a set have the same initial day of release.

You will be able to see how many more stamps you need to complete the particular set. Indeed you will be able to decide whether you will in fact be able to complete the set. It may be that the set in question includes one or two expensive stamps and you may decide that for the time being at least you will ignore these.

Once you have sorted out all the stamps in a set, you may feel able to mount the stamps on a page in your album. Always remember that you should not overcrowd your stamps on the page. Eight to twelve stamps on one page are usually quite sufficient.

Place the stamps to be mounted on the page and move them about until you come across an arrangement that looks attractive to you. It is best to keep the left- and right-hand halves of your page symmetrical. You should also vary the number of stamps in each row to give your page some variety. It is often best to arrange that the longest row of stamps comes about two thirds down the page. If there are one or two stamps in the set which you do not at the moment have, but feel you should obtain them without difficulty in the near future, then leave spaces for them on your page.

Once you have decided on the layout of the stamps on the page, make faint pencil marks to indicate where each stamp will go, so that you will know where to place each stamp when you come to mounting.

If your sets consist of only three or four stamps you might be able to mount about two sets on a page. Try to keep your sets in the order in which they were issued as far as possible.

By the way, when arranging your stamps on the album page, there is no need to keep them in order of denomination. An attractive layout frequently comes from paying more attention to the shape and size of the stamps, and keeping the shapes and sizes balanced.

If for any particular set you are still missing a large number of the stamps but hope to obtain these stamps, it is best to keep those stamps which you do have in a stockbook and add the missing stamps as you acquire them until you are ready to mount the set. A stockbook consists of a number of pages which comprise pockets in the form of transparent strips into which stamps can be slipped for safekeeping. Such books can not only be used to house any stamps that are awaiting mounting, but can also be used to hold your duplicate stamps.

This will be very useful when swapping. You will have your spare stamps with you and will be able to see which stamps are missing from sets.

As already said, if you are specialising, the stamp catalogue will tell you when sets were issued and what denominations are involved, so that you can keep your collection in order.

If you are not specialising, you will be less concerned about dates of issue, or even the completeness of sets. However, it will still be a good idea to keep stamps from the same set together. Although you will be less formal, it is still worthwhile arranging each page of stamps with as much care as indicated previously.

Having arranged your stamps carefully, you may wish to add what is known as 'writing up', that is some written details about the stamps themselves. Such information might be the reason for the issue of the stamps, the date of issue, the name of the person who designed the stamps, the name of the stamp printer and the process used, the watermark and the perforation measurement.

Exactly what information you give is entirely up to you, but do not forget you are building a collection of stamps, not writing a book. Therefore do not include too much writing up.

Writing up can be done in a number of styles depending on your own abilities. You can write freehand or use a stencil. Use a fountain pen, dip-in pen or even pencil (but not ball-point pen—because such pens will not give you a very pleasant-looking final product). You can use a typewriter (be careful) or one of the modern forms of transfer lettering (but this can be expensive).

It is best to write-up your collection before actually mounting your stamps; mounting should be your last process. The final product, of a well-arranged page, with some neat writing up and the stamps carefully mounted, will give you a stamp collection to be proud of.

Designing and Printing Stamps

In this book there is only room to give very basic details about the design and printing of stamps.

It may not have been apparent to you that stamps have to be specially designed, but in fact it is quite a skill. It is necessary to convey a message on what is a very small area of paper. The point of the design has to be easily recognised by those looking at the stamp. Simplicity is very important.

Stamp designers are usually specialists in this particular form of work. When post offices require new stamps they might approach just one recognised stamp designer, or they might request possible designs from a number of designers and then select those they consider to be best.

Stamp designer Patrick Oxenham preparing the artwork for the Great Britain Shire Horses issue (*Photograph by courtesy of the British Post Office*)

It is later up to the stamp printer to reproduce the designer's work as accurately as possible and to produce the thousands of stamps required by a post office.

Those who are interested in stamp printing will find that several books have been written on the subject and about the technicalities involved.

It will be sufficient here just to mention the four basic processes used, so that you will be able to recognise the terms when you meet them in a stamp catalogue, and perhaps recognise stamps printed by the different methods.

Recess or line-engraved printing

This form of printing, which was used for the very first stamps, uses the idea of cutting the design out of a steel plate. When the plate is inked, the ink fills the recesses which have been cut out, so that when the surface of the plate is wiped clean of ink, some ink still remains in the recesses. When the plate is placed in contact with paper, the ink from the recesses is transferred on to the paper, producing the necessary design.

As you can tell, the design on the plate has to be in reverse, so that it will appear the right way on the paper.

You can often tell a recess or line-engraved stamp because the design tends to stand up from the rest of the paper. Run your finger gently over the surface of a recess printed stamp and you will feel the design.

Letterpress

This method is today mostly used for applying an 'overprint' to a stamp. The design to be printed stands up from the rest of the plate (look at the keys of a typewriter—you will see that the letters stand up). The ink is then applied just to the 'raised' design and so when the plate is put into contact with paper, the design is transferred to the paper.

Photogravure

As the name implies this is a photographic method of printing which leaves the paper totally flat. The idea with photogravure is to have a plate which consists of a large number of tiny holes, called cells. These cells differ in depth: the deeper the cell, the more ink it will hold, and the deeper the colour it will print. The reverse is naturally also true. The depth of each cell is very small—thousandths of an inch—and there can be up to 90,000 of the cells to a square inch!

Looking at a photogravure printed stamp under a magnifying glass you will see the design consists of a number of dots, representing the cells, although each of the dots is of the same size.

Lithography

This process produces stamps which might be confused for photogravure. Looking at the stamp under a magnifying glass will show that the design once again consists of a large number of dots, but this time the dots vary

Producing the printing cylinders which are used to print the final stamps

in size. The larger the dots, the deeper the colour which is printed, and vice versa.

The best example of how a picture printed by lithography is built up is to look at a newspaper photograph, for here the pattern of dots, being much larger, will be easier to see.

Normally the lettering on a stamp printed by lithography is not broken down into dots, whereas with photogravure it is still necessary for the lettering to consist of a pattern of dots.

Naturally with all stamp printing methods, when a stamp is printed in more than one colour, a separate printing plate is needed for each colour used.

A lithography stamp printing machine in operation

Stamp printers normally print the stamps on paper which has already been gummed. Sometimes the paper is kept in large reels which are fed through the stamp printing machines, the reels being cut into individual sheets of stamps (comprising any number from five to 400 stamps) after printing. On other occasions the gummed paper is cut into sheets before printing. After the stamps have been printed the perforations are added.

Sheets of stamps being carefully checked to make sure that all are perfect and that no errors escape

Different Types of Stamp

In the previous chapter printing of stamps was mentioned and it was implied that all stamps are printed in sheets. It is certainly true that most stamps are sold by post offices in the form of sheets which comprise a number of stamps ranging from as low as five to as many as four hundred.

Stamps come in other forms however, Stamps sold from vending machines are produced in long strips for this purpose. Such stamps are known to collectors as 'coil stamps'. Stamps can also be bought in book-

A strip of stamps sold from a machine, called a 'coil' strip. Note that this strip has stamps of different denominations joined together, these being said to be 'se-tenant'

lets. Normally each page in a booklet contains about six stamps. Booklet stamps hold a great deal of fascination for stamp collectors because of the way in which they have to be produced. For example a page of stamps in a booklet frequently comprises stamps of different denominations joined together. When two different stamps are issued joined in this way they are said to be 'se-tenant'.

All the stamps so far referred to are what is known as postage stamps, that is they are used to indicate that the postage charge on a letter or parcel has been paid. Other types of stamp also exist.

Stamps are sometimes used for revenue purposes, for example, to indicate that certain legal fees have been paid. In most cases normal postage stamps are also used for such revenue purposes. There have been times when stamps have been specially issued for revenue purposes. Such stamps used for revenue are not usually of interest to stamp collectors. However, if a stamp intended for revenue has been used *postally* (and therefore bears a postmark) it will be of interest to a stamp collector.

Equally a postage stamp used for revenue—you can usually recognise such a stamp because rather than being cancelled with a postmark it will be obliterated by someone's signature—is not of interest to a stamp collector.

A stamp used for revenue purposes

Before condemning such items however it is as well to remember two points. Obviously if a stamp is scarce you may be pleased to have an example in your collection cancelled by a signature until such times as you can obtain a postally used example. Also there is a branch of stamp collecting called 'Cinderella' collecting which is concerned with items which resemble stamps, but which are in fact not postage stamps as issued by a recognised postal authority.

For example, some of the small islands around the coast of the British Isles need to make private arrangements to bring their letters over to the mainland where they can be put into the British postal system. A charge is

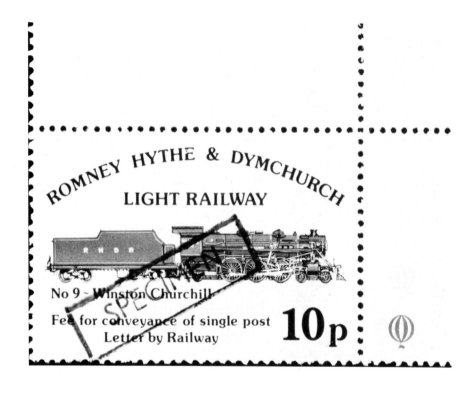

ROMNEY HYTHE & DYMCHURCH
LIGHT RAILWAY

No 9 ~ Winston Churchill

Fee for conveyance of single post
Letter by Railway

10p

SPECIMEN

A stamp issued for local carriage purposes—in this case by a railway. This stamp is
not sold by the British Post Office

made for this private carrying of letters, and 'stamps' are often issued to
indicate that a fee has been paid. Although not a fully recognised postage
stamp as such, these 'stamps' are called 'local carriage labels' and are
collected.

Another type of stamp which you may encounter is that used to indicate that postage is due. Such 'postage due labels' are used to show that

Postage due stamps from Jersey

insufficient postage was paid on a letter or parcel, or that some other charges (such as Customs duty) need to be paid.

As a general guide, if a stamp is listed in a stamp catalogue, then you can be assured that it is a fully recognised postage stamp. If you cannot find a stamp in a stamp catalogue then it is best to seek the advice of another collector. It may be that the stamp has only recently been issued and therefore as yet has not been recorded in the catalogue.

It may however not be a postage stamp at all, although looking very much like such a stamp. A dealer will be pleased to advise you whether or not to put a doubtful stamp into your collection.

Expressions you will Meet

Throughout this book reference has been made to terms used by stamp collectors; there are other expressions you will encounter as you build up your collection. To help you there follows a summary of some of the more important terms.

Advertisements

There have been times when advertisements have been printed on the backs of stamps. You may also find advertisements within some stamp booklets, either on the covers, the inside pages, or even as labels joined to the stamps within the booklet.

Advertisements have appeared on the backs of stamps or on labels attached to stamps

A block of twelve 'Penny Black' stamps showing the alphabet letters in the bottom corners. Note that the letters change from stamp to stamp. This block of stamps was sold by Stanley Gibbons Auctions Limited

Air Mail

Letters which are sent from one country to another by air are said to go by air mail. Many countries issued special lightweight sheets, already stamped, useful for short letters, which are sent air mail. Such sheets are called 'aerogrammes' or 'air letters'.

Alphabet Letters

If you look at the early (Queen Victoria) stamps of Great Britain you will find tiny letters usually in the bottom two corners. These were introduced as a security device and the idea was that each stamp on a sheet would have its own letters. For example, the first stamp in the first row of the sheet would be lettered 'AA'. The second stamp in the first row would be lettered 'AB'. The first stamp in the second row would be lettered 'BA'. The pattern of letters would continue in a similar way. Later, letters also appeared in the top corners in the reverse order to those in the bottom corners.

Block

The name given to a number of stamps joined together. For example you may hear the expression 'a block of four' which would refer to four stamps joined together in two rows of two stamps.

Booklet

A small book which contains a number of stamps, normally those stamps which are in most common postal use, sold by a post office.

Cancellation

A device used to show that a stamp has been used for postage purposes and thus cannot be used again. Sometimes stamps are found to be deliberately cancelled for sale to collectors and have not been on a letter sent through the post. Such stamps are called 'cancelled to order' and many more advanced collectors dislike them because they have not been used for genuine postal reasons. However they do provide a way in many cases of acquiring a large number of stamps at relatively low cost. Always

Two blocks of stamps showing the cylinder numbers (sometimes also known as 'plate numbers'). In one case the cylinder numbers are given as 1B 1B 1B 1B showing that the stamps were printed from four cylinders and therefore in four colours. The second block has the single cylinder number 1 (being a one colour stamp) and also shows the 'Jubilee line' in the bottom sheet margin

70

remember however that such stamps have been cancelled for the benefit of stamp collectors and that genuine postally used stamps are preferable.

Coil Stamps

These are stamps sold from machines and consequently come in the form of strips. Some stamps sold from machines have no perforations down two sides or it will be found that the perforations have been trimmed close to the stamp.

Similar situations can also be found on stamps from booklets, which may have one or two sides without perforations or with perforations which have been trimmed.

Commemorative Stamps

These are stamps issued for a particular reason, such as to honour an anniversary or to mark an event.

Cylinder Numbers

The numbers given by the stamp printer to the cylinder from which the stamps are printed. Frequently such numbers are printed in the margin of the sheet of stamps. (Such numbers will naturally be printed in the same colours as used for printing the stamps. They should not be confused with the 'serial numbers' often printed in black in the sheet margin which are a means of counting the number of sheets printed.) Some Great Britain Queen Victoria stamps can be found with the cylinder (or plate) number incorporated in the stamp design.

Definitive Stamps

These are the stamps in regular use, as opposed to 'commemorative stamps' which normally are put on sale from post offices for a short period of time. The stamps used in Great Britain which feature just the monarch's portrait and the denomination are the definitive stamps.

Error

A mistake made by the stamp printer when printing a stamp. A colour omitted from a stamp printed in several colours, or a stamp without perforations which should be perforated would be examples of 'errors'.

Stamp printers are very thorough in their checking of stamps to ensure that no errors are released to post offices and subsequently to the public. However, with millions of stamps being printed every day it does occur that an occasional error slips through undetected.

See also 'varieties'.

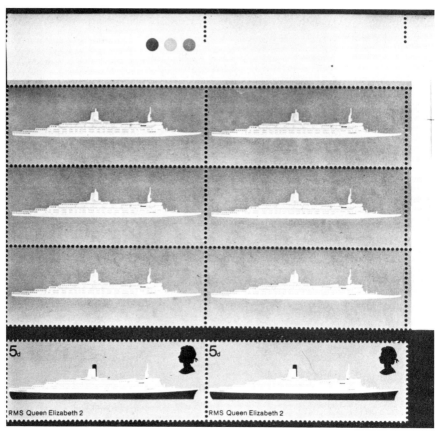

Two errors on stamps. In the first case on this page the black printing is missing from the Great Britain stamp showing the Queen Elizabeth 2. In the second case overleaf the aircraft is printed upside down

Fake or Forgery

While these two terms are different in meaning, they both represent an attempt to artificially create a stamp and/or postmark, which is not the genuine item.

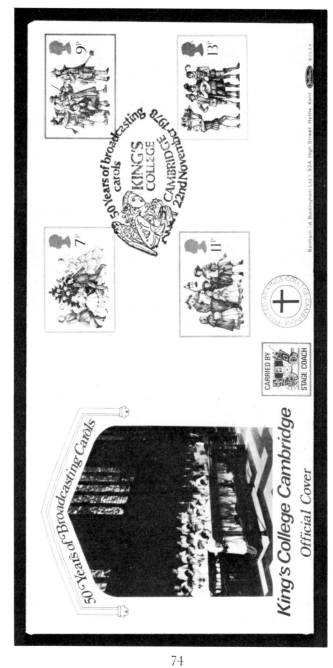

A first day cover

74

First day Cover

An envelope to which a complete set of stamps is stuck and postmarked on the first day of issue of the stamps is called a 'first day cover'. Frequently the envelope is designed to match the stamps; such envelopes are often sold by post offices for use with a new issue of stamps.

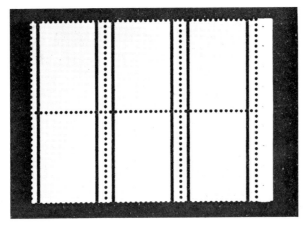

Graphite lines printed on the backs of stamps (these come from a booklet of stamps)

Graphite Lines

For a period of time British stamps were issued with black lines printed on the back as part of experiments to develop machinery which postmarks stamps automatically.

Gum

The adhesive on the back of the stamp by which it is stuck on to an envelope.

Gutters

Many stamps are printed in sheets through the middle of which there is a white unprinted margin (which divides the sheet into two sections). This margin is known as the 'gutter', while a pair of stamps, one on either side of the gutter and joined to the gutter is called a 'gutter pair'.

Pairs of stamps with the 'gutter' between

Handstamp

A form of postal marking, such as a cancellation on a stamp, which is applied by hand rather than by using a machine.

Jubilee Line

The solid line of colour which is often found in the margin of a sheet of British stamps below the bottom row of stamps. These lines are called 'Jubilee Lines' because they first appeared on Great Britain stamps issued in 1887 which was the Golden Jubilee of the reign of Queen Victoria.

Local Stamps

Stamps which are issued to pay for the carriage of a letter purely locally. An example is the stamps applied to letters sent from an offshore island to the mainland to pay the cost of such carriage: such stamps would be known as 'local carriage labels'.

Margin

The area around the stamps when in the form of sheets. Sometimes a text is printed in this margin. Other items printed in the margins include the 'cylinder numbers' and occasionally arrows to help the post office clerks divide each sheet into quarters.

Maximum Card

The name given to a postcard which has a picture which corresponds to the design of a stamp: the stamp should be stuck to the picture side of the postcard and cancelled with an appropriate postmark linking the theme of the stamp and postcard.

The British Post Office issues postcards which reproduce the designs of special stamp issues. These can be used as 'maximum cards' but care should be taken to ensure that Post Office Regulations about such cards are obeyed.

West Highland Terrier

FIRST DAY OF ISSUE LONDON SW

7 FEBRUARY 1978

11P

A postcard with stamp cancelled on the picture side

Miniature Sheet

While most sets of stamps are issued in sheets containing stamps of just one denomination, it frequently occurs that such sets are also accompanied by a 'miniature sheet' which comprise the various stamps of the set printed together to form one small sheet.

A miniature sheet issued by Great Britain

Obsolete

A stamp which is no longer available from the post office of issue is said to be obsolete. A stamp which is no longer valid to pay postage costs is called 'invalid'.

Official Stamps

Sometimes stamps are issued which can only be used by Government Departments. There is usually some indication on the stamps to show that they can only be used for 'official' business, such as the letters 'O.H.M.S.' or more simply 'Official'.

A stamp overprinted with the letters 'O.H.M.S.' for official use

Various forms of overprint: with the word SPECIMEN, indicating that the stamp is intended for publicity purposes and cannot be used for postage; to commemorate a Royal Visit because there was insufficient time to print special stamps designed for the occasion; to indicate a change of currency

Overprints

Sometimes after a stamp has been printed it is necessary to add additional text perhaps to commemorate an event when there is insufficient time to have special stamps printed. Such a text printed on existing stamps is called an 'overprint'.

It has been known for one country to overprint its name on the stamps of another country. For example, before Cyprus issued her own stamps she used the stamps of Great Britain overprinted 'Cyprus'.

Sometimes the overprint is in the form of a denomination. For example, if a country is short of, say, 12c stamps but has plenty of 20c, then some of the 20c stamps may be overprinted 12c and sold as such to make good the shortage. When the overprint changes the denomination of a stamp this is frequently called a 'surcharge'.

A strip of stamps showing normal perforation holes along the top and bottom, but 'rouletting' between the stamps

Perforations

The holes around the edge of a stamp which enable two stamps to be easily separated from one another.

Collectors like to be able to measure the size of the perforation holes and for this purpose use a 'perforation gauge'.

The measurement of a perforation is taken as the number of holes in 2 cm.

There are two basic types of perforation used for stamps. The first is known as 'line perforation'. By this process the tops and bottoms of the stamps are perforated separately from the sides. As a result the perfor-

The difference between line and comb perforations

ations often do not meet exactly at the corners, giving a jagged appearance.

The second method is known as 'comb perforation' by which the top and sides of a stamp are perforated at the same time: this provides the stamp with a neat appearance at the corner.

There are other types of perforation which are generally outside the scope of this book, except to mention 'rouletting', which is a system of slits (rather than holes) by which two stamps may be separated.

Initials perforated into a stamp (normally by a Government department or private business as a security measure) are called 'perfins'.

Phosphor

A colourless substance applied to British stamps (and the stamps of a few other countries) needed to activate the automatic letter cancelling equipment (see also 'Graphite Lines'). Frequently phosphor can be seen as dull bands when looking along the surface of a stamp. The proper way of detecting phosphor is to use an ultra-violet lamp, but such equipment should really only be used by advanced stamp collectors.

Postage Due Stamps

Stamps which are used to denote that further charges are still to be paid on an item which has already passed through the post.

Postal Stationery

Envelopes, postcards and airletters sold by post offices with a stamp already printed on them are called items of 'postal stationery'.

Postmark

A marking applied to an envelope or packet during the course of its passing through the postal system. Most postmarks are used to cancel the stamp so that it cannot be used again. They also frequently provide the time and date the item was posted and the place where it was posted.

Postmarks also frequently carry some form of message, called a 'slogan', such as 'Remember to use the Post Code'.

Two examples of attractive postmarks from France

Most postmarks are applied by machine. (See also 'Cancellation' and 'Handstamp'.)

Many collectors value a postmark applied to a stamp on the day the stamp was issued. An envelope bearing a stamp issue postmarked on the day it was released is known as a 'first day cover'.

Printing

See the separate chapter in this book.

Self-adhesive Stamps

While most stamps have gum on the back which needs to be moistened to attach the stamp to an envelope, some stamps have been issued which are 'self-adhesive'. These are sold with a backing sheet, and the stamps need to be peeled from this backing and then placed straight on to the envelope.

Care should be taken to mount self-adhesive stamps in the album with a backing paper attached (the original backing sheet if the stamp is unused or part of the envelope if it is used), otherwise damage could occur to the stamp and album page.

Two self-adhesive stamps

Se-tenant

Two stamps (or more) of different design, colour or denomination issued joined together are said to be 'se-tenant'. If you obtain some se-tenant stamps it would not be advisable to tear them apart to give you the individual stamps—keep them joined together.

84

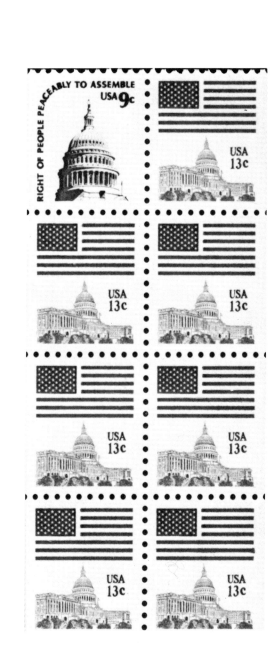

A se-tenant block of stamps

Sheet of Stamps

Most stamps are printed in large sheets which comprise a number of the same stamp.

Occasionally the different stamps which make up a set are issued joined together as a small sheet. This is known as a 'miniature sheet'.

Tête-bêche

Two stamps joined together (se-tenant) with one stamp upside down in relation to the other.

Thematic Collecting

The collecting of stamps by their design rather than the country of issue.

Traffic Lights

Solid circles of colour (one for each colour in which the stamp is printed) which appear on the margins of sheets of stamps to help the printers check that all the colours have been printed correctly.

Unused and Used

A stamp which has not been on an envelope through the post is said to be 'unused'. An unused stamp which has all its original gum and is as issued by the Post Office is said to be 'mint'. A stamp which has been cancelled by the Post Office is called 'used'.

Variety

A slight variation to a stamp caused by a fault on the printing cylinder. As such a particular 'variety' will only be found on one stamp on each sheet, but will be found to occur on that same stamp on every sheet printed, or at least until such times as the fault is corrected.

This differs from an 'error' which normally only affects a single sheet of stamps and all the stamps in that sheet.

Watermark

A device or design incorporated into paper during its manufacture. This design can often be seen by holding a stamp up to a strong light and looking through the stamp. Other methods of detecting the 'watermark' of a stamp were given on page 51.

Enjoy your Hobby

This book has only been able to give you an introduction to the hobby of stamp collecting.

Always remember that you will gain far more from your hobby if you look closely at your stamps, find out as much as you can about your stamps, and do not be afraid to seek the help of others.

Older collectors will be only too pleased to guide you based on their own experience.

Nevertheless always remember that stamp collecting is a personal hobby. It can be developed in the way which gives you the most pleasure and enjoyment.

Happy Collecting!

Useful Addresses

There are a number of organisations which aim to encourage young collectors and school stamp clubs.

If you would like to be put in touch with your local adult philatelic society, contact the Secretary, British Philatelic Federation, 1 Whitehall Place, London SW1A 2HE for the name and address of the secretary; many adult clubs have sections specially for younger collectors. A letter to the same address will bring details of the Melville Junior Stamp Competition, an annual competition for young collectors for which a number of medals are given as awards.

The British Post Office at St Martins-le-Grand, London EC1A 1HQ has a section which helps school stamp clubs. Ask your teacher to write for more information.

The Post Office has a number of fascinating films which are available on hire: the Crown Agents Stamp Bureau, St Nicholas House, St Nicholas Road, Sutton, Surrey, also has film strips available for hire by stamp clubs.

A whole range of services for the young collector and school stamp clubs is available from the Stamp Collecting Promotion Council, 27 John Adam Street, London WC2.